THE BEGINNER'S GUIDE TO DOING BUSINESS IN CHINA

Prizgar Gonzales

I0393498

DEDICATION

To my wonderful wife, VeeLa, for her virtuous and everlasting love.

For my mother Virginia Gonzales who at this writing has celebrated 104 years on earth and whose guiding light is the purifying force that illuminates and protects my life.

Acknowledgements

My wife VeeLa's belief in me as a writer is my guiding grace. She has been there every step of the way inspiring and expressing magnanimous patience as editor.

It is hard to imagine my career as a writer without her respect for the art of prose and an author's isolation.

Her inaudible presence, a gift to behold, as she serenely shares her knowledge as a Tai Chi master to her devoted students.

As I go about my day, I am forever embraced by the unconditional love of my mother, Virginia Gonzales, who at this writing has celebrated 104 years on earth.

To my son Darion and his family, to my daughter Debra and her family, to my brothers and sisters, uncle and aunts, nieces and nephews, VeeLa's family, countless friends and cousins, you are all precious to me.

Special thanks, to my friend Owen Stoby, who with the blessings and support of his family, accompanied me on our first trip to China.

TABLE OF CONTENTS

Chapter 1

CHINA'S LONG HISTORY OF WEALTH

Historically, China has been the world's most successful creator of wealth. Other than the 19th century when Europe dominated the world's economy and the 20th century when the U.S.A. emerged as the richest nation on earth, China savvy and deft, has pervasively prospered without peer.

Former U.S. Secretary of State, Henry Kissinger, in his esteemed best seller, "On China", says, "Not only was the scale of China traditionally far beyond that of the European states in population and in territory; until the Industrial Revolution, China was far richer."

He continues, "As late as 1820, it produced over 30 percent of the world GDP—an amount exceeding the GDP of Western

Europe, and the United States combined." In fact, Kissinger emphatically states, "China produced a greater share of total world GDP than any Western society in eighteen of the last twenty centuries."

On the economic ropes for much of the 19th and 20th centuries, constantly absorbing and fighting off lethal military and economic blows from foreign invaders, China, having patiently survived, is now in cruise control with unprecedented wealth and global economic power.

With the 21st Century now only in its teen years, China has positioned itself as the most productive, educated, self-motivated and energized work force on earth.

Their economy is humming at break-neck speed, energized by a vibrant young population armed with a holistic approach to life, work and career.

With the U.S. becoming more Conservative, and economically coldblooded, as 1% of the population control nearly all of the wealth, a wise and prudent option to secure your own economic wellbeing, is to learn to do business with China.

What China offers is a golden opportunity to build a successful business.

The most surprising aspect of this book is the revelation that starting a business and trading with China is easier than you think. This guide will show you how.

If you are yearning for the freedom to be your own boss and dance to your individual rhythm, China could be your perfect partner.

The Chinese make doing business very easy. The truth is these are people that live, breathe and celebrate business. They enjoy their vocation, whatever it might be, with gratitude, drive and humility.

Frankly, of all the nations on earth, China by far offers the best path for a new business to get started. If, by chance, you have a sketch of a shoe design, getting it manufactured in the U.S.A. is close to impossible.

The business class in the U.S.A. is wrapped in legalism and reluctant to take risks. With China there are no such barriers and stop signs.

One can do business in China for decades and never once have to hire a lawyer. If there is a business problem, the parties involved treat it as a business problem and solve it.

The business highway in China is user friendly and this book will show you how to get in the right lane.

Within these pages you will find a tried and true approach to get onboard as a participant on China's economic juggernaut.

If you have or don't have an idea, a passion, or a dream, China is the place to be. Their economic banquet is so lavish, so layered; you can fill your plate with countless business items, even products that cost pennies.

The Chinese take lightly the American thinking that an idea belongs to only one individual or corporation.

They have no problem or hesitation tweaking a successful brand, idea, or product, by putting your name or brand on it, so you can start a business.

Their mantra, "Of course, no problem." I agree, so don't get trapped by paying patent lawyers or copyright lawyers your hard earned money to protect an idea that someone is going to tweak, modify and improve. Please, free yourself of that burden and expense.

Another major economic asset mastered by the Chinese worker, is his ability to duplicate, copy or clone anything in the marketplace.

It's a national and personal challenge to perfectly duplicate and improve anything that's been made. This national drive is the high-octane that anyone, anywhere, can use to his benefit. You don't have to reinvent the wheel but you can sure tweak it and a source in China will produce it.

These pages are for individuals with or without a plan to initiate a brand, or start-up.

China has a formula that is hard to beat. They have instituted and unleashed a well-trained and sharp government management cadre with a non-confrontational approach to helping businesses expand.

It's a formula that will allow anyone, anywhere, to fire their bosses and take control of their own lives. It's a formula that can enhance your ability, joy, and satisfaction to join the global business community while providing economic security for your self and others.

Chapter 2

PLANTING YOUR ECONOMIC SEED

For some years now, I have been thinking about the outrageously lopsided wealth divide of the U.S.A. Out of a population of over 250 million, approximately 1% own the majority of the wealth.

Many of us seem cornered, fatigued, and burnt-out, trying to figure out what to do about it. For those in that category the American middle-class dream has become a mirage.

Millions of Americans are caught in the unenviable position of banging on the door of the 1% pleading for a job. To this observer, that is self-inflicted modern slavery. Not I.

This book will give you the tools to unshackle yourself and begin your journey on the free enterprise road. Yes, being fearless and directing your initiative toward business ownership.

I have always been mystified and intrigued by Chinese history and culture. But after reading "Adventure Capitalist", Jim Rogers' captivating account of his travels around the world on a motorbike, I concluded from his statements about Asia, that China owned the 21st century.

I decided to further my research and experience China's business offerings first hand.

I wanted to observe, in a concentrated area, what China was producing.

My research led me to the Mother Of All Trade Shows: The Canton Trade Fair.

My friend and business associate Owen Stoby was also looking to shed the manager/caretaker trap.

After a brief discussion, he was immediately on board to make the journey. We also agreed that in order to appreciate all that the Canton Trade Fair had to offer we must take in all three phases.

I had the responsibility of finding the best airfare and hotel deal. On Expedia, the internet travel agency, I found an offer we could not refuse: 22 nights at the Ramada Pearl, in Gaungzhou, plus return flights, for two, on Cathay Pacific, totaling US$3,557.64. Divided by two, my cost was US$1,778.82.

I courageously planted my economic seed, worth US$1,778.82, allowing me 22 days in Guangzhou, China, to take in all three phases of the Canton Trade Fair.

For 22 days, I shared a comfortable business suite and was in a position to observe, close up, China's economic juggernaut while networking with countless business associates from China and around the world.

Today, the economic seed I planted in China has sprouted strong business roots, making way for countless leaves and budding flowers.

Truly, the best investment of your time is nurturing your self-employment and reaping the rewards.

Wasting your time is when you are a manager/caretaker of another man's saga.

Your God given choice is the right to roll your own dice. Only the momentum of freedom's road will take you to a place where you can celebrate the love and the joy that writing your own saga brings.

The stats show that two thirds of millionaires currently working are self-employed. It is that simple, so let's begin.

Chapter 3

The CANTON TRADE FAIR

China is the Land of Trade Shows and the Mother of all Trade Shows is the Canton Trade Fair. This immense trade fair is held twice per year in April and again in October. There are three phases of Canton Trade Fair.

PHASE 1:

* Large Machinery & Equipment
* Small Machinery
* Bicycles
* Motorcycles
* Vehicle Spare Parts
* Chemical Products
* Hardware
* Tools
* Vehicles (Outdoor)
* Construction Machinery (Outdoor)
* Household Electrical Appliances
* Consumer Electronics

* Electronic and Electrical Products
* Computer & Communication Products
* Lighting Equipment
* Building & Decorating Materials
* Sanitary & Bathroom Equipment

PHASE 2:

* Kitchen & Tableware
* General Ceramics
* Art Ceramics
* Home Decorations
* Glass Art Ware
* Furniture
* Weaving, Rattan & Iron Arts
* Gardening Products
* Stone & Iron Products (Outside)
* Household Items
* Personal Care Products
* Toiletries
* Clocks, Watches, & Optical
* Instruments
* Toys
* Gifts & Premiums
* Festival Products
* Native Products

PHASE 3:

* Men & Women's Clothes
* Children's Wear
* Underwear
* Sports & Casual Wear
* Furs, Leather, Down & Related Products
* Fashion Accessories & Fittings
* Home Textiles
* Textile Raw Materials & Fabrics
* Carpets & Tapestries
* Food
* Medicine & Health Products
* Medical Devices, Disposables & Dressings
* Sports, Travel, & Recreation Products
* Office Supplies
* Shoes
* Cases & Bags

Flawlessly executed and managed, the Mother of all Trade Shows is massive but user friendly.

Judging from the three phases every business category or product is represented. You will acknowledge that most of what is consumed daily all over the earth is either made, assembled, packaged or grown in China.

Observe African merchants purchasing exquisitely designed and crafted dinette sets and other high-end products, catering to their fast growing Nuevo Riche.

Even African style textiles, designed and manufactured by Chinese merchants are ready for the asking.

Rich Arabs, their women decked in burkas, revealing only inquisitive and searching eyes, buying everything in sight; from the burkas they are wearing, to modern self-contained desert tents, sleek ATV'S, ginger, garlic, oranges, front doors fit for a modern Taj Mahal, sleek modern stoves, entire bathrooms with enchanting fixtures, champagne, crystal glasses, watches, shoes, every disposable imaginable, etc., etc.

The Indians, witnessing their countries rise and growth, eagerly purchase the heavy construction equipment on display.

Latin Americans are present in great numbers, meticulously negotiating and purchasing for their region's insatiable appetite.

The Germans, still ruling the world with their BMW and Mercedes Benz brands, seemed awed, ceding all other manufacturing to China.

If after you trod through the fair, taking in booth after booth, meeting countless people and manufacturing sources, and you emerge with an English-speaking agent, a passion for a product, or get onboard as a general merchandiser, you are on your way.

Chapter 4

Getting to The Canton Trade Fair

From every corner of the earth, merchants flock to the Canton Trade Fair to indulge and feast at a massive manufacturing banquet.

If you are searching or already have a passion for any of the categories at the Canton Trade Fair, you will find your success under Heaven's Sky. But first, let's show you how easy it is to get into the big dance.

Your first move is to contact your nearest Chinese Consulate and apply for your visa. The visa costs less than US$200.00, allows you multiple entries, and is valid for one year.

If all is well with your application, the form is quite easy, you will get your visa in seven to ten days.

Your choices are to attend all three phases, two phases or one phase which, of course, includes your passion product.

Having decided on your length of stay, and having secured your visa, airfare, and hotel, you have one other important move, which is to obtain your entry badge.

There are two easy and less time consuming approaches to secure your badge. Just show up at the registration desk at the China Import and Export Fair at the Pazhou Complex, 382 Yuejiang Zhong Road in Guangzhou, armed with a passport size photo, your name card and your passport, and you will be taken care of.

Also, at most hotels in Guangzhou, you can get your badge in a few minutes for approximately a US$20.00 service fee. Your badge is valid for all three phases.

Before you leave for China arm yourself with a few hundred name-cards.

The Chinese don't use the term business card. To them it's a name card. There is a protocol in handing someone your name card. Hold your name card with both hands with your info facing the receiver as you make eye contact. You will witness a genuine smile reflected on the receivers face for your courtesy.

Most Chinese retain their family name but nearly all of them have an American first name. You will be introduced to lots of John's, Toms, Sheila's,
Joan's, Jim's, Bill's, Tina's, Cathy's, etc. Their motive, aim, and strategy, is to always please and accommodate the customer.

A week before you depart, contact your hotel in China to confirm your bookings. You can also ask the hotel what is the approximate taxi fare from the airport to your hotel. Be warned, during the Canton Trade Fair the Chinese taxi hustlers come at you like vultures as prices escalate.

The Chinese Yuan Renminbi is the currency of China. In the world of business it is called the RMB and in the streets the Yuan. The exchange fluctuates, as of this writing the exchange averages 6 RMB or Yuan for US$1.00.

The average taxi fare from the airport to the city center is US$25.00 or 150 Renminbi (RMB). To the just landed rookie, the hustlers will offer to take you for 400 RMB or US$66.00. Exercise patience, inquire where the official taxi cue is and all should be OK.

If you are adventurous, and traveling light, you can get to the city center in Guangzhou by subway for 4 RMB or US$0.66.

The subway system in Guangzhou is easy to navigate, ultra-modern, fast, clean, arrives every 3 minutes and has both audio and signage directions in English.

At the airport, the best way to get RMB is by using an ATM. However, and this is very important, contact your credit or debit card provider and notify them of your travel plans to China.

You might find some local ATM's in China not accepting your credit or debit card. Don't worry just find another one. I find that ATM's affiliated with the Bank of China are the best way to go.

Most businesses in China, except major hotels, don't accept U.S credit or debit cards for purchases. So be prepared to pay for nearly all of your purchases with RMB. Also, the hotel where I stayed rejected all of my U.S. dollars with any markings on them. They only exchanged crisp and clean U.S. dollars.

If you have U.S dollars with markings on them that are "old" looking take them to a bank to be changed. In China always carry your U.S passport with you.

Due to the popularity of the Canton Trade Fair, hotels and airfares significantly increase during their show dates.

I suggest searching the Internet and other travel sources a few months in advance for a package deal that fits your needs.

The Chinese economic banquet is not to be missed. It is the rocket fuel that is driving the world's economy and if you step on board it could be the catalyst to your personal economic salvation.

Chapter 5

NAVIGATING The CANTON TRADE FAIR

Most Guangzhou hotels offer courtesy buses to and from the Fair.

On the courtesy bus to the Fair, on the hotel elevators, in the restaurants, gym and lobby, introduce yourself to the interesting mix of nationalities that you will encounter. Some might be rookies like you, but the majority are multi-year veterans with a reservoir of information, tips and priceless suggestions.

If you are using your hotel's courtesy bus, to and from the Fair, ask the driver for the location of your bus for the return trip to your hotel.

For those without a courtesy bus to the Fair, the Pazhou Station stop on Guangzhou Metro Line 8 will get you to and from the Fair.

The Canton Trade Fair is housed at the Pazhou Complex. The architectural design is in a class by itself compared to other Trade Fair buildings around the world. On first sight it's an imposing breathtaking structure. Situated on the banks of the tree lined and serene Pearl River, the design, wide and glistening, flows like a tranquil river with its silver roof illustrating a soothing and welcoming wave.

Be prepared to log countless miles in order to cover the winding pedway of the Canton Trade Fair. However, there is a constant flow of free electric car rides and every 90 meters there are escalators, elevators and stairs.

Carrying a small 4-wheel suitcase is ideal for loading up on all the catalogs, CD's, and other promotional material that will come your way.

To ease your carrying weight, kindly ask the vendor if their company has an informational CD instead of a catalog.

Some company's catalogs, besides being heavy, don't include their latest products, whereas, CD's are lighter and tend to have an updated version of their line.

Although covering an extremely large area, navigating the Canton Trade Fair is very easy. There are countless information booths with friendly and computer savvy English speaking youths at your service.

Large bold signs display well-placed directions. Smoking areas are well situated for those that enjoy lighting-up.

Large food stalls accommodate the ravished and Chinese fast food restaurants visibly dominate. For those that crave American style fast food, the golden arches, pizza brands and KFC are well represented.

Personally, I start the day with a Chinese espresso, which I find intoxicating, and in the afternoon indulge in another.

Enhancing my espresso are the pure angelic smiles wishing you a good day, from the young female college students moonlighting as waitresses.

During the day, I drink a lot of water, complimented by energy bars and a nut mix, until I get to my neighborhood and enjoy a three or four course vegetarian meal.

The atmosphere in the Trade Fair is relaxed with friendly and helpful faces everywhere to assist.

You will be delighted to find the Chinese vendors courteous and approachable, most speak English, and some are very sharp in sizing you up as a serious potential customer.

It is better to be honest and transparent about your intentions. Frankly state that this is your first time experiencing the Canton Fair. This humility will hold you in good standing and you will be invited to have a seat to talk further.

If something is new feel free to ask questions, showing your sincere interest in learning about the product. As you know, knowledge brings opportunity and power.

As you will notice during the three phases of the Canton Trade Fair, China manufactures countless products. If you are fortunate and already have a passion for a product, you can easily get your name or brand on it. The key is to be fearless and smart.

When I went to China I knew not a soul. Twenty-two days later, after taking in the three phases of the Canton Trade Fair, I had met and conversed with business associates from Germany, Botswana, Morocco, India, Houston, South Africa, Antigua, Barbados, Austria, Kentucky, Bahrain, France, etc., etc., made contact with valuable Chinese business sources, found a dedicated Chinese agent, and was blessed with a few new Chinese friends.

Entrepreneurs from all corners of the earth are enjoying China's economic stew. Course upon course is being served so join the feast. It is the fuel that is propelling the world's economy.

I had the pleasure of meeting a number of Canton Fair veterans who marvel at the speed of China's growth.

To keep abreast of all the new cutting-edge innovations on display, these international veterans make their yearly pilgrimage to the Canton Trade Fair. They are constantly searching for creative stimulation.

At the Canton Trade Fair you not only partake in multiple innovations, new ideas, and products on display, but you will be in the enviable position of knowing what's new and hot in the market place.

Chapter 6

Your CHINA AGENT

Getting an agent to represent you in China is crucial to your success. Without an agent you will be playing Russian roulette with your time and your investments. So don't, even for a moment, consider going it alone.

The ideal place to meet a business agent from China is at the Canton Trade Fair. The tried and true approach to find an agent is to ask for a recommendation from a businessperson who has one.

I strongly recommend, when in conversation with any veteran foreign buyer you encounter at the Fair, that you ask them to introduce you to their agent. These veterans were once in your shoes and will willingly assist you. Feel free to ask about their experiences and inquire about any nuances that you should look out for.

Invite the agent to join you for lunch or dinner. This is your opportunity to get to know the agent. Feel free to share bits of your life's story and diplomatically inquire about theirs. Also, ask the agent to state their responsibilities regarding your business.

In my experience, agents in China will take care of nearly all of your business related needs while you are there and diligently communicate with you when you leave.

Cooperation is a respected and honored word in China. By cooperating, all parties strive to become rich which in turn leads to a long mutual friendship.

Most Chinese agents speak English, however, your communication with them must be on a level that you are comfortable with.

When interviewing agents pay close attention to their level of English comprehension. In fact, purposely send the agent you are considering an email requiring detailed answers. In their answer you will be looking for two signs: (a) how long they took to acknowledge receiving your email and (b) their ability to articulate their thoughts and points of view in English.

If you are satisfied with the agent's response-time, and their writing ability in English is coherent, then you have an ace on your business team.

The duty and responsibilities of your agent is multifold. A good agent will monitor and enforce quality control of your product. Which means that your agent must have a good working knowledge of your product line.

In your interview discuss the agent's experience with your product. If your business is heavy construction machinery, you naturally don't want an agent whose specialty is selling hats.

A professional agent will insure that if your order is 10,000 hats all of your hats are the correct sizes, the right fabric, the exact color, the hats are packaged and labeled properly, insured, and meet all necessary certifications and customs requirements before being loaded on to a ship for delivery.

Agents make their money and earn their reputation by being honest, frank, diplomatic and fair. The agent's fee is between 1% and 3%. Truly a bargain considering the agent's fee will be added on to your selling price.

Chapter 7

The MINIMUM ORDER

China has an exciting business formula for anyone, anywhere, to start a business. One significant part of the equation is the minimum order quantity or MOQ. If Americans, and others worldwide, jump on China's MOQ system, free enterprise will reign supreme among the masses.

Hey, the 1%, in every country, has excess gravy for their potatoes and they aren't sharing. So it is imperative that you look out for #1, you.

You must develop and strengthen your will to be your own job creator. Indeed, stop begging for a job and strengthen your will to create your own.

To this observer, a business arrangement with contemporary China is economic salvation. Here is how the MOQ works. If you have a passion for selling women's shoes that's where we are going to start, manufacturing and importing women's shoes from China.

At the Trade Fair, in booth after booth, you are truly impressed by all the beautiful shoes on display.

In aisle, after aisle, the designs and colors have you awestruck. You are surprised and silently take note that the Chinese women love wearing well designed feminine shoes and they wear them well.

You can't help but envision introducing these shoes to potential customers. You are blessed that shoes are your passion and you find yourself surrounded by all the major manufacturers.

You are invited to sit, in booth after booth, with manufacturers to discuss your plans. You are told that it is easy to put your brand on any sample on display. Your other option, you are advised, is to sell the manufacturers brand. The choice is yours.

You can ease into the shoe market by selling the hot brands on display or you can be fearless and introduce your brand to the world.

Outside of the Fair, your market research grows in confidence. While enjoying a stroll on Beijing Road, Guangzhou's trendy shopping strip or a Subway ride, especially on a hot day as millions of beauties in shorts or short dresses, all wearing beautiful shoes, demonstrate that you are on the right track. Your will to succeed is strengthened. Yet, your hot new style still has to hit Main Street, America.

You have walked around for five days at the Canton Trade Fair. You have romanced the countless shoe manufacturers and have been dazzled by all the creativity, colors, and designs.

The manufacturer will gladly put your name brand on any design. Your MOQ is 5,000 pairs of shoes per style and color. You are now faced with the challenge of fulfilling your MOQ. I will show you how easy that can be if you have the passion to succeed.

Just picture yourself as the maestro conducting a symphony of manufacturers, independent sales reps, wholesalers, retail dynamos and others. They are all virtuosos and as the importer/maestro enjoy all their skills. It's your composition so let them play your song. Because after the orchestra plays, as the importer, it will be your duty to pay.

Weaved into the melody are the independent sales representatives with their customers, the wholesalers and retailers. In many ways the independent sales rep makes the melody contagious.

Rest assured that the product you are introducing already has a distribution network in place. The independent sales rep will guide your product to the proper conveyor belt.

In the virtual world you don't necessarily have to have a physical sample to introduce your line and to take orders. A laptop computer, iPad or smart phone will do. Your Chinese supplier, via your agent, will supply you with sharp photos of your preferred shoe styles via email. However, after meeting your supplier in person at the Canton Trade Fair, you will be supplied with physical samples of your shoe line.

The main ingredient necessary for your MOQ success is having independent sales representatives in every region presenting your shoe line to buyers.

If seeing is believing, when the sales rep approaches the USA buyers, they will have a good look at your shoe product and you will be closer to your MOQ goal.

The tried and true doctrine for importers to adhere to is to refrain from buying products from China without committed orders from your market. Beware, you will be tempted, so don't break the rule.

The best way to find independent sales representatives is by spending time in shoe stores in your country getting to know the personnel. Introduce yourself and state that you are in the shoe business. The rest is easy: simply ask for the name and telephone number of their shoe sales rep.

Independent sales reps know each other so if you are based in Chicago ask your Chicago rep to introduce you to their associates in New York and California. By following that pattern your shoe brand will have nationwide representation.

The independent sales rep is fully aware that it is easy to introduce a new brand of shoes to Neiman Marcus, Saks, Macy's, or any other dynamo in the retail business. The fact is, for these retail dynamos to stay on top of their game, they have to execute to perfection, their 80/20 marketing and sales formula. It's a simple formula.

All store's bread and butter is the 80% of their goods that are reorders of the tried and true. The 20% is allocated for folks like you with new products. None of these retail dynamos want to be left out of the possibility that a new product or trend may catch fire with consumers.

The retail dynamos also have a minimum order (MOQ) system. Their MOQ is what keeps them on the cutting edge and aware of any new trends. This is your opening, your ace, to help fulfill your Chinese MOQ.

A professional sales rep will have done the research on the retail dynamo. Their intelligence will show how many outlets this dynamo has and your sales rep will make the pitch to have each outlet store carry the MOQ of your brand.

The other major market under your sale reps jurisdiction is the independent retail store or boutique. There are more independent stores than there are chain dynamos. So your goal to reach your MOQ has improved again.

All I am saying is: be your own job creator. Get to the Canton Trade Fair, meet the suppliers, find a Chinese agent, and return to the USA focused on fulfilling your 5,000 MOQ order.

As a maestro, with a hot melody climbing up the charts, please don't get too excited when you fulfill your first MOQ. The fact is you are only in business when the retail dynamo and others reorder your brand and you have graduated to the tried and true 80%. Truly, by creating a hit, royalties will definitely follow.

Chapter 8

Enjoying The City of Guangzhou

The Canton Trade Fair has three phases with three days off between each phase. You have many choices how to spend your days off. It's your call, but I would advise that you get to know this dynamic city.

While seeking shelter from the rain in a park on the Pearl River, a street merchant insisted on selling me a mechanized gadget that massages your body.

The more I waved her off, not wanting it, the more she massaged my neck, arms, chest, shoulders and back. My refusals only triggered her calm Zen-like effort to make the sale. I wondered about this; if this persistence is ingrained in the business DNA of the streets, then the Chinese are hard to beat economically.

Taxis in Guangzhou are cheap compared to other world cities. My preferred mode of transportation in Guangzhou is the subway. I am in awe at how effortlessly the system carries millions upon millions of passengers daily.

The subway system is ultra-modern, safe, clean, most rides costs US$0.50, English is spoken, and trains arrive every 3 minutes. It is great to be among the masses, to observe and learn, as they go about their daily life.

Guangzhou's weather in April and October, the months of the Canton Trade Fair, always hoovers around 70 degrees Fahrenheit.

In Guangzhou, a city of close to 15 million people, the police don't carry guns. To this observer, that was a pleasant surprise. It is a city where millions are energized by the rhythm of a new day, bobbing and weaving, slicing and dicing. Ancient and modern move in harmony executing their will to succeed.

There is a sense of personalized urgency as the masses are focused on catching the wave of prosperity that millions are already enjoying.

The bicycle takes on the 18-wheeler truck head-on, demanding his rightful slice to maneuver. What's truly amazing is that there is no road rage, no rude outbursts.

This is China so you expect great food for the simple reason that the Chinese have mastered the art of sautéing. Oh, speaking about food, I have a great video on You Tube, "It's Fun Eating In Guangzhou Part 1", based on my eating experiences in Guangzhou.

It's fun being a vegetarian in Guangzhou because it's tropical. In my Guangzhou neighborhood, as all over China, restaurants, retail businesses and food markets abound. In these markets you will find an abundance of fresh vegetables and fruits.

True story: on my first day in Guangzhou, I walked into a crowded restaurant, owned by Chinese Muslims and located in the hood, not in the ritzy or tourist areas. No one spoke any English and the menu was all in Chinese with only words and no pictures.

After trying in vain to order vegetables only, I noticed a refrigerator containing a few plastic bags with vegetables. I approached the refrigerator, opened the door, and to my delight I found four separate bags of tomatoes, carrots, bok choy, and spinach. I retrieved the bags and in sign language indicated that I wanted the vegetables cooked.

The waiter, who I nicknamed "Puerto Rico", took the four bags of veggies behind the kitchen curtain.

A few moments later, a Mongolian looking woman (Mama) totally clothed, except for bulging bright eyes, revealing deep Silk Road roots, rose petal cheeks, and her head covered Muslim style, silently walked by and selected fresh herbs from the refrigerator.

After she disappeared behind the curtain, I heard the woks screaming, Mama Maestro was in romance mode, leaving absolutely no fear or doubt that a five star meal was on its way.

As the tone of the woks screaming escalated, "Puerto Rico" served tea. Whoever mixed those tea leaves together understood the meaning of living Under Heaven's Sky. Delicious. Shortly after, failing to disguise an arrogant and prideful smirk, "Puerto Rico" brought the first course.

I had never eaten sautéed tomatoes as a main course, but Mama Maestro in her genius, blended exotic herbs and spices into a memorable and scrumptious entree.

With Mama's creativity on a pedestal, I decided to randomly test another restaurant, but with a twist. I took the liberty to go to the neighborhood market and purchase the veggies on the way. As I strolled and canvassed the neighborhood restaurant strip, observing the chefs, I ran into "James Dean". He was the one. I dismissed any anxiety and brought my bag of veggies into the restaurant, asking the chef via sign language to prepare them. He agreed. I was truly under Heaven's Sky.

As soon as I saw him, he triggered memories of the reckless sophistication of the late American actor, James Dean. He possessed that rare and envious trait of youth, rebel, artist, restlessness, style and charisma.

His haircut was masculine and modern, jet-black and draped to perfection. James Dean never smiled, and had the gift of drama. Anytime he fetched a cigarette from the pack he roped it around his fingers before gracefully placing it between his lips.

With great style, he twirled the cigarette around and around his lips, like a personal form of meditation, as he surveyed and sized up his patrons, mystically disappearing into his domain to create.

While my business associate, Owen Stoby and I, waited we ordered a large bottle of Pearl River beer.

Across the room were two French sounding men. I introduced myself. Surprisingly, they happened to be vegans. I was annoyed with myself for stereotyping the French as carnivores.

Their food arrived first and I was truly impressed by the exquisite presentation of immaculate looking golden carrots garnished with red and yellow peppers, while on another plate, red jalapenos caressed cauliflower, and onions. The crowd was now in a festive mood with laughter and drinks flowing freely knowing that "James Dean's" culinary delights were on the way.

Chewing slowly, I silently gave thanks for having two superb vegetarian dining choices, a perfect way to unwind and dine after long days at the Canton Trade Fair.

After dinner we walked to the late night fruit market for our favorite dessert: the water from freshly cut coconuts and fresh squeezed sugarcane juice.

Chapter 9

YOUR CUSTOMS AGENT

As an importer, you will be lost in space without a customs broker. So it is imperative that as soon as you return to your country you make inquiries, get a recommendation, and introduce yourself to a customs broker.

What is great about customs brokers is that they willingly give you free unabridged information. Every piece of merchandise must clear customs before you can take ownership. They are naturally in your corner making sure all of your papers are in order for your goods to be cleared and unloaded at a port.

With the customs broker in charge your merchandise will smoothly arrive at your warehouse or garage. Every category of merchandise that enters a country has rules, regulations and tariffs. With the customs broker you receive that information for free.

Your goal is to work with the customs broker to insure that your goods flow through the system without any hiccups. All i's must be dotted and all t's must be crossed.

Make a habit of asking your customs broker to answer any import related questions. Again, the advice is free. For example, if during your day you happen to come across an unfamiliar term like "surety bond", the customs broker will freely clarify. This knowledge is vital to your success.

These folks are daily clearing the Red Sea on your behalf. They get paid approximately US$150.00 per hour. Regardless if your merchandise is worth US$100.00 or US$1,000,000.00, their rate remains the same.

All freight on a steamship line and all duty owed to the U.S. Customs Service require separate payments. Consult with your customs broker about whether they will handle both transactions on your behalf.

A Consumption Entry Form must be filled out for all merchandise entering the U.S.A. This means that the customs broker has to be paid to bring this document into existence on your behalf. Learn about the bill of landing and maritime insurance. Your answer is a telephone call away.

Ask your customs broker for a "full rate" or an "all in" rate. This will allow you to know in advance all of your charges. Any charge applicable to your merchandise you must know about. There is no reason not to know. The "full rate" or an "all in one" will reveal it all, including any "currency adjustment factors" or C&F.

When the steamship line converts your payment into a foreign currency it might find the rates unfavorable to them. In order for the steamship line to break even, adjustment charges may apply. By working with your customs broker you will have no surprises.

Speaking about surprises, you will be stunned at how cheap it is to get a shipment from China via ocean freight. Once your agent in China has hooked you up with the best supplier to produce your goods the cost of shipping them to your garage or warehouse will be miniscule.

Chapter 10

YOUR ROLE And VALUE

As an importer let me explain how sweet your value is in the market place. The secret lies in the 80/20 retail buying equation.

Retailers spend 80% of their time looking for innovative people like you. Why? Because their customers are always asking the storeowner, "What's new?"

The storeowner has no choice but to contact the independent sales rep and they in turn contact you to help keep the marketplace interesting with exciting products.

The customers are picking up the tab. They are always asking the storeowner, "What's new?" Take a bow, anytime the "What's new?" or "What's next?" questions are raised; your melody is being hummed.

The melody that you bring to the market place is the quality of your work. Only by having a passion for a product can you produce quality. It pays to be good at what you do.

A start-up company should be lean, no fat. If an expense does not generate business, choose not to spend.

Your value does not rest in how attractive your name card is.
Your value rests in having earned the reputation for producing quality goods.

Spending money on a fancy logo is not going to impress the seasoned professional. Their experienced eye will immediately discern that you are wasting money on non-essentials.

Consider bringing on board a designer from your local community college. Students are always looking to enhance their portfolios and they can be paid through royalties from sales. A great fit for both parties.

When building a company your main concern is fostering relationships.

Be proud of being a start-up. That pride will allow those that have been in your shoes to willingly shower you with tips, advice, leads, and mentorship.

Your value goes up when you can provide the retailer's everyday need for new innovation and quality.

Your supplier in China honors you for allowing their company to grow by providing a new market. All parties: your Chinese agent, customs broker, independent sales rep, designer, etc., etc., have perfectly played their stanzas and are very pleased with their maestro, you, holding the band together.

Be genuine, confident and optimistic. On the telephone, via emails, or in person, you have the power to inspire all who you encounter during your business day.

Your purpose is to be successful at what you do and to always aim to conduct doing business in a celebratory manner.

Chapter 11

FINAL WORD

China has dramatically changed the business of manufacturing.

The new kid on the block, armed with brand new factories, is rendering obsolete the industrial dinosaurs that once supplied the world with material goods.

Once booming industrial towns in the U.S.A. and Europe are rapidly dying unable to keep up as the Chinese manufacturing dragon wags its globe shaped tail knocking down and reshaping the face of the 21st Century.

The Chinese have proven time after time that there is no safe haven for exclusivity. They have an uncanny ability to observe a product and then manufacture and offer that product faster and significantly cheaper.

No industry or product is immune.

In the 21st Century, to economically survive, you must have the ability to trade in the market place, and what better to trade than your own brand.

I have often wondered why someone with a master's degree in business knocks on another man's door asking for a job.

Why would a master in business not behave like a master and start his or her own business.

The cold 21st Century reality, due to the shrinking job market, is that many of those currently armed with a master's degree in business are forced to become self-employed.

As you learnt in my book if you have or don't have a passion or a dream China's economic banquet is so lavish, so layered, you too can initiate your own business. Have a successful journey!

AIRLINE NOTES

AIRLINE NOTES

AIRLINE NOTES

AIRLINE NOTES

AIRLINE NOTES

HOTEL NOTES

HOTEL NOTES

HOTEL NOTES

HOTEL NOTES

HOTEL NOTES

PRODUCT NOTES

PRODUCT NOTES

PRODUCT NOTES

PRODUCT NOTES

PRODUCT NOTES

MANUFACTURES NOTES

MANUFACTURES NOTES

MANUFACTURES NOTES

MANUFACTURES NOTES

MANUFACTURES NOTES

CHINA AGENT NOTES

CHINA AGENT NOTES

CHINA AGENT NOTES

CHINA AGENT NOTES

CHINA AGENT NOTES

CUSTOM AGENT NOTES

CUSTOM AGENT NOTES

CUSTOM AGENT NOTES

CUSTOM AGENT NOTES

CUSTOM AGENT NOTES

SALES REP NOTES

SALES REP NOTES

SALES REP NOTES

SALES REP NOTES

SALES REP NOTES

NOTES

NOTES

NOTES

NOTES

NOTES

NOTES

NOTES

www.ingramcontent.com/pod-product-compliance
Lightning Source LLC
Chambersburg PA
CBHW061513180526
45171CB00001B/166

* 9 7 8 1 4 8 0 1 9 8 9 9 9 *